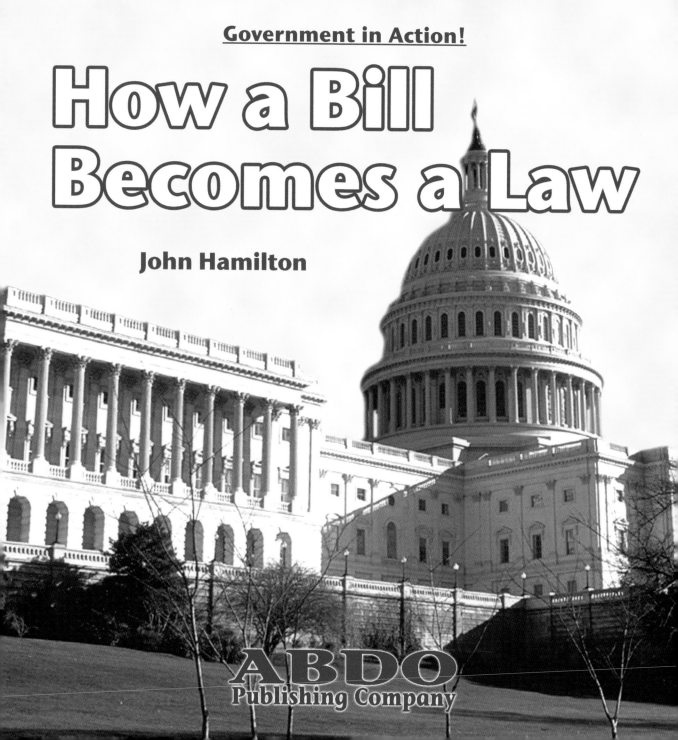

Government in Action!

How a Bill Becomes a Law

John Hamilton

ABDO
Publishing Company

visit us at
www.abdopub.com

Published by ABDO Publishing Company, 4940 Viking Drive, Edina, Minnesota 55435.
Copyright © 2005 by Abdo Consulting Group, Inc. International copyrights reserved in all
countries. No part of this book may be reproduced in any form without written permission from
the publisher. The Checkerboard Library™ is a trademark and logo of ABDO Publishing
Company.

Printed in the United States.

Cover Photo: Getty Images
Interior Photos: Corbis pp. 1, 5, 7, 8, 9, 11, 13, 15, 23, 24, 25, 31; Getty Images pp. 4, 17, 18, 21;
    Photo Edit pp. 28, 29

Series Coordinator: Kristin Van Cleaf
Editors: Jennifer R. Krueger, Kristin Van Cleaf
Art Direction & Maps: Neil Klinepier

Library of Congress Cataloging-in-Publication Data

Hamilton, John, 1959-
    How a bill becomes a law / John Hamilton.
        p. cm. -- (Government in action!)
    Includes index.
    ISBN 1-59197-646-4
    1. Legislation--United States--Juvenile literature. 2. United States. Congress--Juvenile
literature. [1. Legislation. 2. Law. 3. United States. Congress.] I. Title. II. Government in
action! (ABDO Publishing Company).

    KF4945.Z9H36 2004
    328.73'077--dc22

                                                                            2003069305

Contents

What Are Laws?

A boy learns about laws while he is fingerprinted during a field trip.

"Stop in the name of the law!" This phrase is often heard on television. But what does it mean? What are laws, and why are they important?

Laws are sets of rules that societies use to govern. These rules are meant to protect people. They also **guarantee** people's rights. Laws make communities better by helping citizens live together peacefully.

There are two main branches of law. Criminal laws deal with actions that harm society as a whole. People who break these laws can be punished with fines, imprisonment, or even death. Civil laws have to do with individual citizens. They deal with contracts, property ownership, and repayment for personal injuries.

There are many laws in the United States. While laws cover many different areas, they still have something in common. They all begin as ideas outlined by bills. Every day, U.S. lawmakers work to turn these bills into laws that benefit the American people.

Who Makes Laws?

In the United States, the federal government creates and maintains the nation's laws. The government is made up of the executive branch, the legislative branch, and the judicial branch. Each branch keeps the other two from becoming too powerful. But, they all play a part when it comes to the nation's laws.

The legislative branch creates laws. Article I of the Constitution created a two-**chamber** legislature. These chambers are the Senate and the House of Representatives. The House of Representatives is sometimes simply called the House. Together they are called Congress.

The Senate is made up of 100 members. Each state has two senators. They are elected by the people in their home states. Senators serve six-year terms. The Senate's **presiding officer** is the vice president. If there is a tie vote, the vice president can cast the deciding vote.

Opposite page: *Congress meets in the Capitol in Washington, D.C. The House of Representatives and the Senate meet on the second of the five floors. The House chamber is in the south wing, and the Senate chamber is in the north wing. Visitors may watch House or Senate sessions from third-floor galleries.*

The House of Representatives has 435 members. They are called congresspeople or representatives. The people in each state elect their representatives. The number of representatives depends on the state's population. All congresspeople serve two-year terms.

Representatives stand during the opening session of the House of Representatives.

The Speaker of the House is the **presiding officer** of the House of Representatives. Other members of the House elect this person. The Speaker presides over House **sessions** and gives representatives permission to **debate**. He or she also appoints House members to joint committees.

The executive branch enforces the laws passed by Congress. This branch is led by the president. Many departments and agencies, such as the Department of the Treasury, help the president in this duty. These groups create regulations and other acts that carry out laws.

The judicial branch of government makes sure laws follow the Constitution. It consists of the federal courts, including the U.S. Supreme Court. Like the executive branch, the judicial branch doesn't create laws. But, the courts do make decisions about laws that affect many Americans.

Types of Legislation

Congress has a number of duties, but its main job is to make laws. It does this by **debating** and passing bills. A bill is a document that outlines the details of a proposed law.

There are two types of bills. Public bills affect everyone. Private bills affect an individual or an organization. Both kinds are used for different purposes. For example, authorization bills create government programs, and **appropriation** bills fund them.

Congress carries out other types of business as well. It issues joint resolutions, which can also become laws. Congress uses them to gain appropriations for certain projects. They require approval from both **chambers** and the president. Joint resolutions are also used to make changes to the Constitution.

Congress may also issue concurrent resolutions. These resolutions make or change rules that apply to both chambers. They are also used to express the opinion of the entire Congress. Unlike bills or joint resolutions, concurrent resolutions do not become laws.

Congress can also pass simple resolutions. These resolutions deal with issues within the individual **chambers**. They are used when the Senate or House wants to make new rules for its chamber only. And, they can give the opinion of just one house. Simple resolutions do not become laws.

The joint congressional resolution that officially declared war on Japan in 1941

How Bills Start

Congress deals with bills every day. But where do ideas for bills come from? Often, senators and representatives develop them. Sometimes, Congress members are acting on campaign promises. Or, they may know of issues in their home state.

Congress itself also develops ideas. Congressional committees research certain issues in the country. They look into the details and causes of problems. Then, committee members can suggest laws to fix the issues.

The president is aware of issues in the nation as well. The president has the duty to report to Congress. He or she may make suggestions for legislation. However, the president cannot personally introduce a bill. It must be introduced by a senator or representative.

A Congress member's **constituents** have ideas, too. Citizens often know the details of many issues affecting them. They use their right to **petition** the government to suggest ideas for bills. This way, the people play a part in their government and the laws that govern them.

Margaret Chase Smith was the first woman to be elected to both houses of Congress. And in 1964, she became the first woman to campaign for presidential nomination.

Introducing a Bill

Once a member of Congress has an idea, he or she needs to prepare the bill. This person may work with lawyers in the House or Senate legislative counsel's office. The member may also try to gain support from other House or Senate members.

Anyone can submit a proposal for a law. But only a member of Congress can introduce it. This person is called the sponsor. Additional supporters are called cosponsors. Identical bills may be introduced in the House and Senate at the same time. They are called companion bills.

To introduce a bill, House representatives put the proposal in the **hopper** on the clerk's desk in the House **chamber**. Senators may give the bill to a clerk at the **presiding officer**'s desk. Or, they may stand in front of the Senate and formally introduce the bill.

Next, the clerk assigns the bill a number. Bills introduced in the House of Representatives have the letters *H.R.* in front of the number. In the Senate, the number is preceded by an *S.* This introduced version of the bill then goes to the chamber's presiding officer.

Bills can start in either chamber. However, bills to raise money must start in the House. Here, Congressman Richard Nixon introduces a bill by placing it in the hopper.

Committees

When the **presiding officer** receives the introduced version, he or she then refers it to a committee. The committees are smaller groups of Congress members. Each committee deals with bills that cover specific subjects. Each **chamber** has its own number of permanent committees.

Many of the committees have one or more subcommittees. These smaller groups examine certain types of bills within the committee's subject. Bills are often sent to subcommittees, but not always.

Committee members carefully examine the bills that are sent to them. They decide whether to act on the bill. Only about 15 percent of bills are acted on. The rest are tabled, or killed. This means the bill will not go any further.

If the committee decides to act, it will usually send the bill to the executive departments and agencies related to its topic. The agencies research the possible effects of the bill. They report back to the committees on the importance of passing the law.

Secretary of Defense Donald Rumsfeld (center) testifies before the Senate Armed Services Committee in Washington, D.C.

If it is decided that the bill is important, the committee will hold hearings. For hearings, Congress asks people to give testimony for or against a bill. Most of these hearings are open to the public.

If the committee decides to make changes to the bill, it will do so in a markup **session**. The committee **debates** certain sections and makes any changes, which are called amendments. If a subcommittee has acted on the bill, it reports it to the full committee. The full committee may further study the bill.

When the bill is written in its final form, the committee takes a vote. If the members decide to table it, no further action is taken. Otherwise, they report the bill to the entire House or Senate with the recommendation that it be passed. This is called the reported version of the bill.

Once the bill is reported, it is put on a **calendar**. The House has five calendars, while the Senate has two. In the House, the Committee on Rules then decides what rules the House must follow during debate. The rules must be approved by the full House. Now, Congress is ready to debate the bill.

Opposite page: *Federal Reserve Board chairman Alan Greenspan testifies at a hearing before the House Committee on Education and the Workforce.*

Debating & Voting

The reported version of the bill next goes to the **chamber** floor for **debate**. During debate, members can ask to amend the bill. In the House, amendments must be related to the bill's topic. But in the Senate, senators are allowed to suggest **riders**.

After the debate, the full House or Senate votes on the bill. A majority of members must be present in order to vote. In the House, a majority is 218 members. In the Senate, it is 51.

There are several voting methods. In a voice vote, the members in favor of a bill say "yea" together, and then those opposed say "nay." They may also vote by division, where those in favor stand and are counted, followed by those opposed.

Another system is the roll call, or recorded vote. In this method, how each member votes is recorded. In the Senate, each member says "yea" or "nay" when his or her name is called. In the House, members use an electronic system. They place their identity cards in a machine and make their choice.

Senator Olin Johnston stands behind his 750-page filibuster speech. Johnston wrote the speech in 1957 in an attempt to block a bill from being passed.

Senate Debates

In the House of Representatives, the Committee on Rules decides how much time will be allowed for debate. But in the Senate, unlimited debate is allowed. Senators sometimes use this to their advantage. They will keep talking to keep a bill from being voted on. This is called a filibuster. In the past, senators have filibustered by reading the phone book or by endlessly requesting that the presiding officer take attendance for the Senate. Filibustering will usually continue until either three-fifths of the Senate votes for cloture, or a limit on debate, or the Senate gives up on passing the bill.

The Other Chamber

If a bill passes one **chamber** of Congress, it is a good sign. However this approved, or engrossed, version still has a long way to go. It next goes to the other chamber of Congress. For example, if the bill first passes in the House, it then goes to the Senate.

Once the bill goes from the House to the Senate, it is called the referred-to-the-Senate version. The bill usually follows the same route as in the House. It may be sent to committee. The committee can approve the bill as it is. The committee can also suggest changes, or even reject the bill.

If the bill passes the committee, it is sent to the Senate floor. There it is **debated** and voted upon. If it passes, this engrossed-with Senate version is returned to the House. At this point, the House may approve the bill or make more changes.

The House may also request a conference committee. This committee is a group of House and Senate members that works to compromise on the differences between the bill versions. The compromises must be voted on again by both chambers. If they can't reach an agreement, the bill dies.

The Senate debates a bill in 1940, while citizens watch from above.

Presidential Action

Once a bill passes both houses of Congress in identical form, it is called the endorsed version. At this point, the Speaker of the House and the vice president must sign it. Then, the endorsed version of the bill is sent to the president.

President John F. Kennedy signs the Nuclear Test Ban Treaty in 1963.

The president must approve or reject the bill within ten days. If the president approves the bill, he or she signs it and it becomes a law. If the president does nothing within ten days, the bill also becomes law.

If the president rejects the bill, he or she can **veto** it. The bill is then returned to the **chamber** where it began with a message stating why it was vetoed. Congress may then rework the bill. Or it may pass the law anyway, if two-thirds of each chamber votes to override the president's veto.

A bill can be killed one other way. A **session** of Congress may end less than ten days after a bill is sent to the president. If the president has not signed the bill by the time the session ends, it dies. This is called a pocket **veto**.

Sometimes when the president signs a bill into law, there will be a signing ceremony. The ceremony is held at the White House. People important to passing the law often attend. Finally, everyone's hard work has turned a bill into a law.

A bill can become law without the president's signature. However by not signing the bill, the president is indicating that he does not completely agree with the law.

How a Bill Becomes a Law

An idea is developed for a new law. A representative or senator drafts and introduces a bill.

The bill is sent to committee and subcommittee for hearings and markup.

In the House, the bill goes to the Committee on Rules. In both chambers, it is put on a calendar. Then the full chamber debates and votes.

The bill is sent to the other chamber for committee and subcommittee hearings and markup.

Both chambers vote on the compromises. The Speaker and the vice president then sign the endorsed version of the bill.

The endorsed version of the bill goes to the president to be signed or vetoed. If not vetoed, the bill becomes law.

The second chamber puts the bill on a calendar. This chamber debates and votes on the bill and then returns it to the first chamber.

The first chamber votes on any changes. If the chambers' versions don't match, a conference committee works out the differences.

Once a Bill is Law

Laws are a basic part of any society. They give people a way to peacefully settle problems with others. Without laws, people would be free to do whatever they pleased, including harming others. The people would have no protection. A society without laws would not have the order it needs to run smoothly.

In the United States, the Constitution and the Bill of Rights give the country this order. The federal government supports the ideas in these documents by passing and enforcing laws. The rights and protection these laws provide are some of the benefits of being a U.S. citizen.

Students learn about the law through a mock trial.

Children practice good citizenship by obeying a crossing guard and traffic laws.

Laws apply to all citizens. By obeying laws, good citizens realize all Americans share the same rights. For example, people do not want to have belongings stolen from them. So in return, good citizens would not steal from others.

By respecting the laws, good citizens are protecting themselves and others. In this way, they are also supporting the government that protects them. This support allows the United States to continue as a successful **democracy**.

Glossary

appropriation - money officially set aside for a specific use.

calendar - in Congress, a list that schedules bills awaiting action.

chamber - a legislative or judicial group. A chamber is also a hall where this group meets.

constituent - someone who allows another person to represent him or her.

debate - to discuss a question or topic, often publicly.

democracy - a governmental system in which people vote on how to run their country.

guarantee - to make sure or certain.

hopper - any of various containers for the temporary storage of something.

petition - to make a formal request to a person of authority.

presiding officer - a person who directs or controls a group.

rider - an amendment to a bill that is unrelated to the topic of the bill. Congress members use riders to make a bill either more or less attractive in a vote.

session - a meeting or series of meetings where a government body conducts business.

veto - the right of one member of a decision-making group to stop an action by the group.

Web Sites

To learn more about how a bill becomes a law, visit ABDO Publishing Company on the World Wide Web at **www.abdopub.com**. Web sites about the legislative process are featured on our Book Links page. These links are routinely monitored and updated to provide the most current information available.

Index